GW00838343

THE PREPPER SURVIVING EMP ATTACKS, SOLAR FLARES AND GRID FAILURES

Written By

David Meade

Published by:

eBookIt.com
365 Boston Post Road, #311
Sudbury, MA 01776

First edition - October 2017

publishing@ebookit.com
http://www.ebookit.com

Copyright 2017, David Meade
ISBN: 978-1-4566-2934-2

Table of Contents

THE PREPPER'S GUIDE TO SURVIVING EMP ATTACKS, SOLAR FLARES AND GRID FAILURES

THE SOLAR STORM AND THE NUCLEAR EMP

Imagine if a solar storm the size of the 1859 Carrington Event struck our modern society? Delicate wires run everywhere nowadays. Filaments, computer chips, hard drives, cell phones and electrical lines exist that stretch thousands of miles. Have you stopped to think about your vehicle's computer system? But first, let's talk briefly about a man-made version of the Perfect Solar Storm – the nuclear EMP event.

It has recently been revealed that North Korea has a satellite with EMP capability that in fact passes over the continental US twice daily. This threat is well-known to Congress.

According to the 2004 Commission to Assess the Threat to the United States of EMP Attack (Executive Report),

"Several potential adversaries have or can acquire the capability to attack the United States with a high-altitude nuclear weapon-generated electromagnetic pulse (EMP). A determined adversary can achieve an EMP attack capability without having a high level of sophistication."

It goes on to briefly address the effects:

"EMP is one of a small number of threats that can hold our society at risk of catastrophic consequences.

EMP will cover the wide geographic region within line of sight to the nuclear weapon. It has the capability to produce significant damage to critical infrastructures and thus to the very fabric of US society…"

The Commission's chairman has testified that within one year of such an attack, 70% to 90% of Americans would likely be dead from such causes as disease and violence. The EMP blast itself is not destructive to human beings. It is the aftereffects. It is also highly plausible that many Americans would die of starvation due to the interruption of the nation's food supply.

According to the Washington Department of Health, Office of Radiation Protection, "A 1.4 Megaton bomb launched about 250 miles above Kansas would destroy most of the electronics that were not protected in the entire Continental United States." By the way, this includes the entire electrical grid, much of manufactured with Chinese parts.

So, as you can see, both a massive solar storm or an EMP event could quite possibly end civilization as we know it. I know that sounds drastic, but in the United States and other technologically-advanced countries, how would the mass population handle a prolonged event with very little or quite possibly no electricity? As the Commission noted, our society is utterly dependent on our electrical grid for everything:

- Trucking and transportation

- Gas stations and refineries
- Information and communications
- Commercial production of food
- Water purification
- Most of our military capability

These are only a handful of things that we take for granted because they are always there. If the gas stations were out of order and no refineries were able to produce more fuel, can you imagine how quickly our "civilized society" would break down? With that event alone, grocery store shelves become empty within a matter of days and farmers can't transport any goods. If you were not aware, grocery stores do not stock much extra produce or food "in the back of the store." In order to maintain a high profit margin, stores maintain only a few days' worth of staples until another shipment arrives. This allows them to conserve space and keep overhead lower.

Once the gas stops flowing and the shelves are wiped clean, how long will your neighbor remain civil?

Several tests and scenarios have shown that cell phones will be one of the first tell-tale signs of an electromagnetic event because of the enormous percentage of the population carrying one. If the power grid were to simply go down, this wouldn't affect your cell phone. Depending on your location, your local cell towers probably have back-up power systems, as well.

However, the cell towers, backup power and your cell phone will ALL be disabled after an electromagnetic event, offering you a clue as to what has just happened.

In effect, the government has taken actions that are both counterproductive and what few positive actions they have taken, such as the Deep Underground Military Bunkers (DUMBs), serve to protect only "the elite." Since the government has done absolutely nothing to protect you, you have to protect yourself. This serves as a chilling reminder that no preparations have been made.

Remember: one EMP burst and the US goes dark.

What if an X-60 solar flare leaps from the sun? The coronal mass ejection (CME) heads straight toward Earth. What will happen? How much warning will we have?

The CME is a slow-moving cloud of charged particles. It is accompanied by an X-ray burst. Both have devastating effects. The X-ray burst travels at the speed of light and would reach Earth's surface in eight minutes.

The result

The X-rays would affect all Earth-orbiting satellites in line of sight. GPS communications would go down, and so would communications satellites. That would be your first warning and an obvious signal to those watching.

This would be a one-two punch. The second would be the CME (arriving 1-3 days later) that would cause transformers (which operate with copper wiring) to heat up and overload. As design capacity is overloaded, they burn up.

What then happens to the nuclear power reactors?

Most reactors require electricity to operate the cooling systems. Huge levels of radioactive fuel are on-site. Cooling on a continuous basis is the only way to prevent a meltdown.

This apocalyptic scenario is probable, if not guaranteed. If the reactor cores are not continuously cooled, a catastrophic reactor core meltdown and fires in storage ponds for spent fuel rods is the imminent result.

Nuclear meltdown?

With a widespread grid collapse, in just hours after the backup generators fail or run short of fuel, the reactor cores melt down. Within a couple of days without electricity, the water bath over the spent fuel rods will "boil away" and the stored fuel rods will melt down and burn.

Transformers are made to order and custom-designed for each installation. They weigh as much as 300 tons and cost more than $1 million. Given that there is currently a two-year waiting list for a single transformer (due to recent demand from China and India, lead times have grown to three years), you can begin to grasp the implications of widespread transformer losses.

The Nuclear Regulatory Commission only requires one week's supply of backup generator fuel at each reactor site. The public will have one week to prepare for Armageddon.

Space impacts

Major Ed Dames was part of a CIA and Pentagon jointly-sponsored project involving remote viewing. He stated that this project saw the "End of Days" as being tied to a series of major solar flares over a one-year period. Earth was totally unprepared.

In a recent interview, he was asked whether an asteroid (Wormwood) may have been the cause of the solar activity and flares that devastate the earth. He was not certain but implied it was possible.

The military knows about it – serious researchers know about it. We are facing environmental risk and destruction on a scale we've never seen before. The world is drifting along. The question is, are you prepared?

Classifications of solar flares

The highest-impact solar flares normally experienced are X-Class flares. M-Class flares have a tenth the energy and C-Class flares have a tenth of the

X-ray flux seen in M-Class flares. The more powerful M and X-Class flares are often associated with a variety of effects on the near-Earth space environment. Y-Class exist; however, they are off the charts.

Hole in Earth's magnetosphere

You probably know about the hole in the ozone, but do you know about the hole in the magnetosphere? Governor Jesse Ventura did an excellent show on this.

The area around Earth that extends beyond the atmosphere is called the magnetosphere. The magnetosphere begins at approximately 1,000 km and extends thousands of kilometers into space. The sun and Earth's magnetic field create this layer.

NASA has discovered (THEMIS mission) that Earth's magnetic field contains a hole, which is 10 times larger than they previously believed. The magnetosphere shelters us from solar flares, but the hole is now four times the size of Earth.

The risk

The worst-case scenario would happen when a violent CME that accompanies a Y-Class solar flare would both come at us in a 1-2 sequence. A Y-Class solar flare would send the part of the earth exposed to it back to the 1850s. It would have an EMP effect on all circuitry and electronics. Only hardened military electronics would survive.

Effects of Y-class solar flares

An EMP, or Electromagnetic pulse, is generated from the detonation of a nuclear device and also by extreme solar activity, such as that which was experienced in the year 1859. In the late summer of 1859, a great solar storm hit the planet. This storm was the product of a coronal mass ejection from the Sun.

On September 1 and 2, 1859, Earth's inhabitants experienced the greatest solar storm in recorded history. It was called the Carrington Event. This storm short-circuited telegraph wires and caused massive fires. The typical light show you can watch in the far north, known as the Aurora Borealis, was seen as far south as Cuba, the Bahamas and Hawaii. Spark discharges even set the telegraph paper on fire. The electrical grid at that time was in its infancy, consisting mainly of a few telegraph wires in larger cities. This event, though frightening to those who witnessed it, had no major impact on the society of that day.

If a tremendous amount of energy in the form of a solar flare or a coronal mass ejection occurs from our sun, this represents an explosive burst of very hot, electrified gas that has a mass that exceeds that of Mount Everest.

This time events will be different. The event will bring down the electrical grid and the shelves on the grocery stores will be cleaned out inside of a day. Banks and ATMs don't work without electric current.

Gas pumps won't be functioning. Food transportation will stop. Rioting and looting will be unrestrained. Communications satellites will be down. The 911 function on your phone isn't going to work. For as long as it lasts, until new transformers can be built or imported, society will be in chaos.

THE PENTAGON KNOWS

It is increasingly obvious that the power players in the Pentagon have known about space impacts and the massive climate changes they will cause since at least the 1980s.

Let's look at other evidences:

- Deep Underground Military Bases around the country, and the world
- The government stockpiling strategic food and ammunition supplies
- The new Office of Homeland Security
- Black ops budgets and trillions missing from the Pentagon

This leads us to another topic:

Project Wormwood Learmonth Solar Observatory in Australia

Wormwood and its entourage are clearly listed in the Book of Revelation:

"The third angel sounded his trumpet, and a great star, blazing like a torch, fell from the sky on a third of the rivers and on the springs of water - the name of the star is Wormwood." – Revelation 8:10-11

If you were one of the heads of the US military, and had foreknowledge of specific future space impacts and what direction it was coming in from, and you wanted to study the incoming asteroids what would you do? You'd go down to the southern hemisphere – Australia - and start a military observatory project there with their government.

You just might name the sub rosa observation post **Project Wormwood**.

Here's the official description of Project Wormwood:

"Established in 1979, it is jointly managed by the US and Australian governments. It is staffed by four different organizations - the US Air Force Weather Agency, the US National Oceanic and Atmospheric Administration, the USAF 15th Communications Squadron (Maintenance), and the Australian IPS Radio and Space Services. It is a real-time space weather patrol observatory that monitors the near space environment."

The word 'Wormwood' is mentioned Eight times in the bible; Deuteronomy 29.18, Proverbs 5.4, Jeremiah 9.15 and 23.15, Lamentations 3.15 and 3.19, Amos 5.7 and the last time is in Revelations 8 verse 11.

The debris surrounding Wormwood will decimate one third of the oceans, and one third of the ships. The sea will also sweep over land masses, destroying ships both at sea and at port.

Revelations 8, 8 – 9: "And the second angel sounded, and as it were a great mountain burning with fire was cast into the sea: and the third part of the sea became blood; and the third part of the creatures which were in the sea, and had life, died; and the third part of the ships were destroyed."

Project Wormwood may be one of the most obviously revealing government programs we can discover.

THE IMMINENT EMP THREAT

There are 4 countries and several orbiting satellites that can and probably will cause an imminent EMP event over America.

The four countries are Iran, North Korea, Russia and China. I consider the two top candidates Russia and North Korea. It's Russia who has provided North Korea with EMP weaponry. North Korea has satellites that pass over the U.S. mainland daily. We don't know what's aboard those satellites. It well could be EMP weaponry.

Russia of course has ICBMs capable of launching EMP weaponry. If launched over the South Pole, we have virtually no tracking and no defense. All of our radars look at vectors from the East and West Coast, and to the North. We have been taunting Russia lately and actually for some time. A provoking incident may not even be needed.

North Korea has an unstable leader. While most of his population is starving, he eats cheese imported from France. He has the fourth largest Army in the world. He has nuclear capability. He's a dangerous and unpredictable man. An EMP attack would be a perfect way for him to unleash his military might. The reason you see so many of their rockets explode mid-flight is that they are testing EMP weaponry.

He might even be able to do it in a way that is untraceable – for example, from a container ship. All it takes is one missile that explodes high over Kansas. The U.S. electrical grid goes down. Welcome to 1851. 90% of the U.S. population would not have sufficient food or water distribution.

The North Korean regime has a satellite that is regularly passing over the mid-United States. We've had years to prepare and done absolutely nothing – that is, the government has done nothing. The American people are totally unprotected.

Personal survival preparation should be immediate. World tensions are at an all-time high. The event is imminent. Check out this video for more information:

https://www.youtube.com/watch?v=t67WVDbIdvo

THE IMMINENT EMP THREAT – PART II

The EMP Commission that was established by Congress to assess the threat of an EMP attack has reported that our national electric grid and other U.S. Critical infrastructure will be significantly disrupted by a sudden and high-intensity energy field burst. This could come from a solar flare incident, or from an ICBM, satellite or container-ship launched single nuclear warhead detonated above Kansas.

If a sole EMP warhead is detonated 300 miles into the atmosphere above the middle of the U.S., the continental United States electrical grid (48 states) would go down for months and maybe years. 90% of the population would be affected. Food and water distribution would halt. Emergency services would be virtually nonexistent.

There exist over 2,000 extra high-voltage transformers that need to be hardened. To replace them after a catastrophic failure is impossible – the lead time on order is 12-18 months, and they are manufactured overseas. Here's a quote from their study:

"The first misconception is that only major nuclear powers, such as Russia and China with high yield thermonuclear devices could effectively execute an EMP attack. In fact, low yield devices obtained by emerging nuclear powers such as North Korea and Iran can produce catastrophic EMP effects.

Misconception two, that a nuclear EMP attack would burn out every exposed electronic system. In fact, based on government tests, we know that smaller self-contained, self-powered systems such as vehicles, handheld radios, and disconnected portable generators are often not affected.

My note: If a vehicle survives with its electrical system intact, it still cannot run without fuel, which is pumped through electrical current.

Misconception three, EMP effects on critical infrastructure will be limited to nonsevere, nuisance-type affects. In fact, wide area failure of just a few systems, could cause cascading infrastructure collapse, in highly interconnected networks. One example is the 2003 electric blackout of the northeast was precipitated by a single high-voltage line touching a tree, and then proceeded to cascade to the entire northeast."

The Department of Defense says that EMP protection for civilian infrastructure is DHS's responsibility. And then when I talk to DHS, I get answers that the protection should be done by the Department of Energy, since they are the infrastructure's sector-specific agency. Who's on first here?

Dr. Peter Pry, wrote in The Wall Street Journal, "The Pentagon was wise to move NORAD back into Cheyenne Mountain, but how are the American people to survive?"

In Congressional Hearings he said:

In the midst of that crisis North Korea orbited a satellite over the south pole that passed over the territory of the United States on the optimum trajectory and altitude to both evade our national missile defenses, and, had that been a nuclear warhead, to place an EMP field over all 48 contiguous United States that would have had catastrophic consequences. That was the KSM 3 satellite; that satellite stills passes over us with regularity.

The Department of Homeland Security, the Federal agency responsible for protecting the American citizens, is not doing enough to lead an interagency effort to mitigate the impact of an EMP event, leaving vast populations of Americans vulnerable to the effects of an EMP. The only group that would be totally unaffected is the Amish – quite an irony.

A recent cost study by the Foundation for Resilient Society shows that significant EMP protection could be achieved for an investment in the range of $10 to $30 billion. That is not exorbitant. A failure would cost trillions, and likely impact hundreds of millions of lives.

I would highly recommend to all readers that you Tweet, link, share in social media or email this data to your representative in Congress. It is high time action was taken.

THE EMP EFFECT – SOLAR FLARES

On October 28, 2003, an X-45 massive solar flare was emitted by the sun. It barely missed earth. If it had collided it would have caused trillions of dollars of damage to the electrical grid. Airlines that flew over the pole diverted their routes to lower altitudes. The Japanese ADEOS II satellite was knocked out.

There are significantly different effects of an EMP caused by a nuclear blast and an EMP caused by a solar event. EMP weapons can trigger massively high bursts of gamma radiation (called E1 and E2). Electromagnetic pulses have three components: E1, E2 and E3. E1 and E2 create gamma rays knocking electrons out of the atoms in the stratosphere, which becomes an electrical conductor due to ionization. This can cause field strength of 50,000 volts per meter.

This type of radiation can cause commercial aircraft to completely power down and their computers fail. It affects phones and cars. Tests have shown that 5% of all cars will have permanent damage, another 15% will stall and up to 70% will have dashboard anomalies. This type of blast will cause computers to fail. The transformers in our electrical grid will be incapacitated.

However, an E3 blast (solar flare) will damage the components in electrical conductors, such as power line transformers. The electrical grid goes down, as with the other type of blast. But phones, cars and computers are not immediately affected. The damage from E3 in modern systems is also called quasi-DC currents. Transformers are not designed to handle direct currents.

With a solar flare, you've got temporary usage of your phone, car and computer. But your car will only last as long as you have fuel in it. Service stations pump gas by electricity, and there will be none. Your phone will last as long as it is charged, and that's over with. Your computer will boot up, but there won't be an Internet to connect to.

A solar flare thus moves the country back to 1850, but in gradual stages. It does provide you with more time to react, though. I would recommend driving your car to the nearest general store (don't try a major supermarket, as that will be havoc). Buy food and water for at least one month for starters. Buy two gallons of water per day per person. Stock up on flashlights and batteries. Buy any medicine you need. Well in advance buy water purification tablets at a camping store. The solar flare at least gives you a chance.

But once we leave the realm of commonly known, publicly sourced physics, we enter the speculative area when it comes to EMP super-weapons. We don't know the details because they are classified. But there have been claims that such weapons exist that can generate electric fields of 200,000 volts per meter. This would destroy all of our in-space assets as well. This would send us in one fell swoop back to a 1800s agrarian age. In either case the answer is immediate preparation and developing knowledge.

THE KILLSHOT SCENARIO

Major Ed Dames has a kill shot theory and in my opinion it is based on a large object passing between the Earth and the Sun. He was head of a Project Stargate, which can be researched at the link through the CIA FOIA search engine. It was passed on from the DIA to the CIA in 1995.

From his own website:

What is the Killshot?

During the top-secret Remote Viewing (RV) CIA and U.S. Army research program, trained viewers that were normally tasked with foreseeing the outcome of war related events began picking up on a future occurrence that appeared to mark a dramatic shift in global life. At first, these viewers, along with Major Ed Dames, the program's senior operations and training officer, had feared their subconscious was foreseeing nuclear war. It turns out after years of Remote Viewing sessions, the event is in fact a series of solar flares that are so devastating to the Earth, and they may cause the death of billions and change life on Earth as we know it.

Normally, one might not take such a warning seriously, but what sets this prediction apart from others is that Remote Viewers have a track record of being amazingly accurate regarding globally recognized disasters and events. In fact, there are many predictions that were announced on national radio and TV programs that have already accurately come to pass with unprecedented accuracy including the tragic disaster in Japan, a mysterious crop fungus, the predicted Indonesian 9.0 earthquake and more!

Let's briefly review some of his recent statements:

He is stating that Russia has restarted their remote viewing program. He states Russia and China are attempting to replace the petrodollar.

He claims the secret to surviving the kill shot is to generally be away from cities - fresh water is a key to survival.

Small groups that have enough skill trades (such as doctors and engineers) will survive and prosper.

He believes the western pacific coast will become sterile, and that mass movement of people in this area will move inland.

In earthquake zones, he states things will be very bad.

Multiple solar flares will damage our grid. Solar energy affecting our Earth core will lead to massive weather changes.

He believes the US Northeast will not be an area that survives mainly because of nuclear power plants failing.

The best preparation is education and reading, and having a strategic relocation plan at the right time. There is no end to education.

This may be our final warning from an independent source.

"The truth is incontrovertible. Malice may attack it, ignorance may deride it, but in the end, there it is." – Winston Churchill

STRATEGIC RELOCATION

When chaos arrives you do not want to be located anywhere near a large city. These are hotbeds for crime, rioting and looting. You need a plan to be in place to be quickly relocated from any large metropolitan area, such as Los Angeles, New York City, or Chicago.

The most dangerous metropolitan areas for earthquakes include San Francisco and Oakland, the entire Los Angeles basin, Anchorage, Alaska and of course Seattle, Washington.

Next, you want to Google a "map, nuclear power plants, US" and you'll come up with some good results. Most of the nuclear power plants are on the east coast and in the northeast corridor. There are very few out West. Stay at least 100 miles away from these facilities.

In terms of coast preparation, I'd recommend 150 miles from the Southern, Eastern and West Coasts and an altitude of at least 600-750 feet above sea level. That's tsunami protection.

If you're interest in non-U.S. relocation, and many are, you should consider the beautiful country of South Africa and most of the southernmost countries of South America. This shouldn't include Paraguay – it's an unstable country with a history of rule by dictatorship. But the balance of the major countries, including Brazil,

Ecuador, Peru, Chile and Argentina, all deserve your study and research. You can achieve a major savings on cost of living in some of these countries.

New Zealand and Australia are very expensive for relocation, and there are a lot of milestones that must be met in order to qualify for inclusion in their country. European countries, including Ireland, Italy and Switzerland are much, much more expensive than the U.S.

We all have access to decades of historical data. And really, most people know the facts. Just about everyone has access to websites where they can research the Third Secret of Fatima (Planet X), the Ararat Anomaly (Noah's Ark), and all of the volcanoes, earthquakes and strange weather occurring all over the world today. Most people know that over 100,000 3 plus size quakes have happened in 2016. The challenge is to connect the dots correctly, and then take strategic action.

Let's end with a couple of quotes that say it all:

"If there was a Third Vision of Fatima in which the coastlines of the world fall to terrible violence from the oceans, and millions and millions of people died, surely the talk of such topic isn't something to be desired."

Pope John Paul II, speaking in dark speech and revealing the Secret of Fatima:

"Something is approaching the earth and it will drastically change our world."

Father Malachi Martin, on the John B. Wells show

EMERGENCY SURVIVAL MEDICINE

Prescription antibiotics are not always the answer. Let's look at a series of natural antibiotics that can be used for specific purposes – they have long storage lives, and do not require a doctor visit.

First, let's examine Black Elderberry. This herb grows on many continents – including North America, Europe, and Western Asia. Laboratory tests during 2005 at a London research group included findings that Black Elderberry is 99% effective against the Avian Flu virus. In fact, during the flu epidemic in Panama during 1995, Elderberry juice was used to treat people with the flu.

Elderberry enhances the immune system by boosting cytokine production. These proteins are messengers within the immune system that regulate response. In fact, ingredients with Elderberries have more antioxidants than either vitamin C or E. According to the University of Maryland Medical Center, Elderberry decreases swelling in mucous membranes and relieves nasal congestion.

In summary, Elderberry juice has very strong antiviral effects – the berries contain proteins that effectively prevent viruses from entering the cells. Years ago, I was staying at the house of someone with the flu, and I felt symptoms attacking me. I went to the local CVS, bought Black Elderberry juice, and within one day I felt fine, and as well I never came down with the flu.

Colloidal silver is well known but not too widely tested. However, in 2011 the NIH took 100 children under 12 who were suffering from the common cold. One group was treated with a solution of colloidal silver and beta glucan, and the second group with a saline solution. 90% of the people in the colloidal silver group recovered quickly.

Colloidal silver is silver atoms that are suspended in distilled water. The particles of silver are small enough to move on a cellular level. They destroy pathogens – including but not limited to parasites, viruses and bacteria.

Silver also promotes rapid healing of tissue. In fact, most burn centers use a form of silver and silver-soaked bandaging for burn victims. You can buy colloidal silver at your local health food store.

Colloidal silver has also been used with high success to combat MRSA infections. These are staph infections that can be fatal – they are currently resistant to antibiotics. It's usually incurred during a hospital stay or in athletic settings.

In the early 20th century, western medicine used silver as its primary antibiotic. After the 1930s, antibiotics became the treatment of choice.

However, as more antibiotics were created, the microbes began evolving into resistant strains. In addition, the antibiotics caused major digestive problems. Antibiotics can actually lower immunity by destroying the good bacteria. In fact, some fluoroquinolone-based antibiotics have permanently crippled those who have taken them.

However, silver apparently acts by stifling the pathogen's enzymes that are necessary for survival. Therefore pathogens cannot develop a resistance to silver.

Non-paradigm thinking has to accompany our preparations. We are one minute to midnight.

GEODESIC DOME HOMES FOR SURVIVAL

A man named Buckminster Fuller saw the creative power of the Geodesic Home in 1951. That was the year he patented the geodesic dome, the most energy efficient and structurally safe building system in the world.

Fuller was an engineer, a historian and a philosopher. He was aware of the danger of conventional construction techniques against Mother Nature's issues. He discovered that the sphere is actually the most efficient shape. It covers the highest square feet of living area with the most minimal amount of surface area. A dome home has 30% less surface area, resulting in 30% less spending on the average cooling and heating bill.

A dome house also uses 1/3 less lumber to build than a box house. Despite the use of less material, the dome house is five times stronger than a rectangular house.

Disaster-Proof

These homes are also virtually disaster-proof. During an earthquake in the Santa Cruz mountains back in 1989 (7.1 on the Richter scale), 500 conventional homes were damaged with the need of extensive repair, or they were totally destroyed. The only home to survive that earthquake was an Oregon Dome geodesic dome home.

Why do these homes survive tornadoes, earthquakes and hurricanes when average homes are destroyed? It's the intrinsic strength of the design – the triangle is the strongest shape in building on the planet.

The design possibilities provide for an open floor plan – you can have walls anywhere. Since a dome house is independent of the interior framing, you don't have to be concerned about "load-bearing" variables. Dome homes provide natural openings for large views and windows, letting in the highest level of light possible.

Dome homes look amazing. You will be surprised by the possibilities once you investigate this spectacular building option. To sum up, here are the advantages:

- No load-bearing interior walls – it stands up to earthquakes and hurricanes

- Immense strength

- Great for the circulation of air and heat

- Many dome homes are prefabricated, resulting in low construction costs

- The prefab elements are small and light weight, making them easily transportable

- Heat pressed softwoods and other materials used are cheaper than regular construction

- Because the dome is built of multiple layers – the frame, an interior panel, insulation, the outer shell and skin and so forth – you can employ inexpensive materials for your environment

- Aesthetic appeal – a highly restful and airy environment with amazing acoustics

POPE JOHN PAUL II WARNS OF IMMINENT DISASTER

The October 1981 issue of the German magazine Stimme des Glaubens reported on a discussion that Pope John Paul II had with a select group of German Catholics in November of 1980. The following is a verbatim report of the discussion:

He was asked, 'What about the Third Secret of Fatima? Should it not have already been published by 1960?'

Pope John Paul II replied:

"Given the seriousness of the contents, my predecessors in the Petrine office diplomatically preferred to postpone publication so as not to encourage the world power of Communism to make certain moves. On the other hand, it should be sufficient for all Christians to know this: if there is a message in which it is written that the oceans will flood whole areas of the earth, and that from one moment to the next millions of people will perish, truly the publication of such a message is no longer something to be so much desired."

Another interesting Catholic prophet, St. Malachy (Bishop of Armagh) in 1139 had an audience with Pope Innocent II. During this time, he had a vision of 112 future popes in order. He described each one with a short phrase. For example, the 111th pope was true to the Order of St. Benedictine (this is of course Pope Benedict, who chose this particular name for himself). The last pope is number 112; this just happens to be Pope Francis. St. Malachy said that during his reign a time of unparalleled destruction will affect the earth.

EMP SPECIFICS

STATEMENT OF PETER VINCENT PRY, CONGRESSIONAL EMP COMMISSION, CONGRESSIONAL STRATEGIC POSTURE COMMISSION, AND EXECUTIVE DIRECTOR OF THE TASK FORCE ON NATIONAL AND HOMELAND SECURITY

Thank you for this opportunity to testify at your hearing on the threat posed by electromagnetic pulse (EMP) to critical infrastructure.

Natural EMP from a geomagnetic super storm, like the 1859 Carrington Event or 1921 Railroad Storm, and nuclear EMP attack from terrorists or rogue states, as practiced by North Korea during the nuclear crisis of 2013, are both existential threats that could kill 9 of 10 Americans through starvation, disease, and societal collapse.

A natural EMP catastrophe or nuclear EMP attack could blackout the National electric grid for months or years and collapse all the other critical infrastructures— communications, transportation, banking and finance, food and water—necessary to sustain modern society and the lives of 310 million Americans.

EMP is a clear and present danger. A Carrington-class coronal mass ejection narrowly missed the Earth in July 2012. Last April, during the nuclear crisis with North Korea over Kim Jong-Un's

threatened nuclear strikes against the United States, Pyongyang apparently practiced an EMP attack with its KSM–3 satellite that passed over the U.S. heartland and over the Washington, D.C.-New York City corridor. Iran, estimated to be within 2 months of nuclear weapons by the administration, has a demonstrated capability to launch an EMP attack from a vessel at sea. The Iranian Revolutionary Guard Navy commenced patrols off the East Coast of the United States in February.

NUCLEAR, NATURAL AND NON-NUCLEAR EMP

An electromagnetic pulse (EMP) is a super-energetic radio wave that can destroy, damage, or cause the malfunction of electronic systems by overloading their circuits. EMP is harmless to people biologically, passing through their bodies without injury, like a radio wave. But by damaging electronic systems that make modern society possible, that enable computers to function and airliners to fly for example, EMP can cause mass destruction of property and life.

A single nuclear weapon detonated at high altitude will generate an electro-magnetic pulse that can cause catastrophic damage across the entire contiguous United States to the critical infrastructures—electric power, telecommunications, transportation, banking and finance, food and water—that sustain modern civilization and the lives of over 300 million Americans. Nature can also generate an EMP causing similarly catastrophic consequences across the entire contiguous United States— or even across the entire planet—by means of a solar flare from the Sun that causes on Earth a great geomagnetic storm. Non-nuclear weapons, often referred to as radio frequency weapons, can also generate an EMP, much more limited in range than a nuclear weapon, that can damage electronics, and could cause the collapse of critical infrastructures locally, perhaps with cascading effects over an area as large as a major city.

Any nuclear warhead detonated at high altitude, 30 kilometers or more above the Earth's surface, will generate an electromagnetic pulse. The immediate effects of EMP are disruption of, and damage to, electronic systems and electrical infrastructure. EMP is not reported in the scientific literature to have direct harmful effects on people. Because an EMP attack would detonate a nuclear warhead at high-altitude, no other nuclear effects—such as blast, thermal radiation, or radioactive fall-out—would be experienced by people on the ground or flying through the atmosphere. However, because modern civilization and life itself now depends upon electricity and electronics, an EMP attack is a high-tech means of killing millions of people the old-fashioned way—through starvation, disease, and societal collapse.

Gamma rays, and the fireball from a high-altitude nuclear detonation, interact with the atmosphere to produce a super-energetic radio wave—the EMP—that covers everything within line-of-sight from the explosion to the Earth's horizon. Thus, even a relatively low-altitude EMP attack, where the nuclear warhead is detonated at an altitude of 30 kilometers, will generate a damaging EMP field over a vast area, covering a region equivalent to New England, all of New York, and half of Pennsylvania. A nuclear weapon detonated at an altitude of 400 kilometers over the center of the United States would place an EMP field over the entire contiguous United States and parts of Canada and Mexico. The EMP generated by a nuclear weapon has three components, designated by the U.S. scientific-technical community E1, E2, and E3.

E1 is caused by gamma rays, emitted by the nuclear warhead, that knocks electrons off of molecules in the upper atmosphere, causing the electrons to rotate rapidly around the lines of the Earth's magnetic field, a phenomenon termed the Compton Effect. The E1 component of nuclear EMP is a shockwave, transmitting thousands of volts of energy in mere nanoseconds of time, and having a high-frequency (short) wavelength that can couple directly into small objects, like personal computers, automobiles, and transformers. E1 is unique to nuclear weapons and is too fast and too energetic to be arrested by protective devices used for lightning.

The E2 component of a nuclear EMP is comparable to lightning in its energetic content and medium (milliseconds) frequency and wavelength. Protective devices used for lightning are effective against E2.

E3 is caused by the fireball of a nuclear explosion, the expanding and then collapsing fireball causing the Earth's magnetic field to oscillate, generating electric currents in the very large objects that can couple into the low frequency, long (seconds) wavelength part of the EMP that is E3. The E3 waveform can couple directly only into objects having at least one dimension of great length. Electric power and telecommunications lines, that run for kilometers in many directions, are ideally suited for receiving E3. Although E3 compared to E1 appears to deliver little energy, just volts per meter, this is multiplied manifold by power and telecommunications lines that are typically many kilometers long, building up E3 currents that can melt Extremely High-Voltage (EHV) transformers, typically designed to handle 750,000 volts. Small electronics can also be destroyed by E3 if they are connected in any way to an E3 receiver—like a personal computer plugged into an electric outlet, which of course is connected to power lines that are ideal E3 receivers, or like the electronic servo-mechanisms that operate the controls of large passenger air-liners, that can receive E3 through the metal skin of the aircraft wings and body.

Protective devices used for lightning are not effective against E3, that can build up energy sufficient to overwhelm lightning arrestors and bypass them through electrical arcing.

EMP and its effects were observed during the U.S. and Soviet atmospheric test programs in 1962. The 1962 U.S. STARFISH nuclear detonation—not designed or intended as an EMP generator—at an altitude of about 400 kilometers above Johnston Island in the Pacific Ocean, surprised the U.S. scientific community by producing EMP. Some electronic systems in the Hawaiian Islands, 1,400 kilometers distant, were affected, causing the failure of street lights, tripping circuit breakers, triggering burglar alarms, and damage to telecommunications. In their testing that year, the Soviets executed a series of nuclear detonations in which they exploded 300 kiloton weapons at approximately 300, 150, and 60 kilometers above their test site in South Central Asia. They report that on each shot they observed damage to overhead and underground buried cables at distances of 600 kilometers. They also observed surge arrestor burnout, spark-gap breakdown, blown fuses, and power supply breakdowns.

In the years since 1962, the U.S. scientific and defense community established incontrovertibly, by means of nuclear tests and EMP simulators, that an EMP attack could have catastrophic effects by destroying electronic systems over broad regions—potentially over the entire contiguous United States.

Because so much information about EMP was largely classified for so long, myths abound about EMP that the EMP Commission has endeavored to correct in its unclassified reports and briefings. For example, a high-yield nuclear weapon is not necessary to make an EMP attack. Although a high-yield weapon will generally make a more powerful EMP field than a low-yield nuclear weapon, ALL nuclear weapons produce gamma rays and EMP. The EMP Commission found, by testing modern electronics in simulators, that ANY nuclear weapon can potentially make a catastrophic EMP attack on the United States. Even a very low-yield nuclear weapon—like a 1-kiloton nuclear artillery shell—will produce enough EMP to pose a catastrophic threat. This is so in part because the U.S. electric grid is so aged and overburdened, and because the high-tech electronics that support the electric grid and other critical infrastructures are over 1 million times more vulnerable to EMP than the electronics of the 1960s.

SUPER-EMP WEAPONS

The EMP Commission also found that, contrary to the claim that high-yield nuclear weapons are necessary for an EMP attack, that very low-yield nuclear weapons of special design can produce significantly more EMP than high-yield nuclear weapons. The EMP Commission found further that Russia, probably China, and possibly North Korea are already in possession of such weapons. Russian military writings call these "Super-EMP" nuclear weapons, and credibly claim that they can generate 200 kilovolts per meter—many times the 30 KVs/meter attributed to a high-yield (20 megaton) nuclear weapon of normal design. Yet a Super-EMP war-head can have a tiny explosive yield, perhaps only 1 kiloton, because it is specially designed to produce primarily gamma rays that generate the E1 electromagnetic shockwave component of the EMP effect. Super-EMP weapons are specialized to generate an overwhelming E1, and produce no E2 or E3 but do not need to, as their E1 is so potent.

In 2004, credible Russian sources warned the EMP Commission that design information and "brain drain" from Russia had transferred to North Korea the capability to build a Super-EMP nuclear weapon "within a few years." In 2006 and again in 2008, North Korea tested a nuclear device of very low yield, 1–3 kilotons, and declared these tests successful. South Korean military intelligence, in open-source reporting, independently corroborates the Russian warning that North Korea is developing a Super-EMP nuclear warhead. North Korea's proclivity to sell anything to anyone, including missiles and nuclear technology to fellow rogue nations Iran and Syria, makes Pyongyang's possession of Super-EMP nuclear weapons especially worrisome.

Another myth is that rogue states or terrorists need a sophisticated intercontinental ballistic missile to make an EMP attack. In fact, any missile, including short-range missiles that can deliver a nuclear warhead to an altitude of 30 kilometers or more, can make a catastrophic EMP attack on the United States, by launching off a ship or freighter. Indeed, Iran has practiced ship-launched EMP attacks using Scud missiles—which are in the possession of scores of nations and even terrorist groups. An EMP attack launched off a ship, since Scuds are common-place and a warhead detonated in outer space would leave no bomb debris for forensic analysis, could enable rogue states or terrorists to destroy U.S. critical infrastructures and kill millions of Americans anonymously.

NATURAL EMP – THE END OF CIVILIZATION

Mother Nature can also pose an EMP threat. The Sun emits solar flares and coronal mass ejections that can strike the Earth's magnetosphere and generate a natural EMP in the form of a geomagnetic storm. Geomagnetic storms rarely affect the United States, but regularly damage nations located at high northern latitudes, such as Canada, Norway, Sweden, Finland, and Russia. Damage from a normal geo-magnetic storm can be severe. For example, in 1989 a geomagnetic storm over Canada destroyed the electric power grid in Quebec.

The EMP Commission was the first to discover and report in 2004 that every hundred years or so the Sun produces a great geomagnetic storm. Great geomagnetic storms produce effects similar to the E3 EMP from a multi-megaton nuclear weapon, and so large that it would cover the entire United States— possibly even the entire planet. Geomagnetic storms, even great geomagnetic storms, generate no E1 or E2, only E3, technically called the magnetohydrodynamic EMP.

Nonetheless, E3 alone from a great geomagnetic storm is sufficient to end modern civilization. The EMP produced, given the current state of unpreparedness by the United States and every nation on Earth, could collapse power grids everywhere on the planet and destroy EHV transformers and other electronic systems that would require years to repair or replace.

Modern civilization cannot exist for a protracted period without electricity. Within days of a blackout across the United States, a blackout that could encompass the entire planet, emergency generators would run out of fuel, telecommunications would cease as would transportation due to gridlock, and eventually no fuel. Cities would have no running water and soon, within a few days, exhaust their food supplies. Police, Fire, Emergency Services and hospitals cannot long operate in a black-out. Government and industry also need electricity in order to operate.

The EMP Commission warns that a natural or nuclear EMP event, given current unpreparedness, would likely result in societal collapse.

THE CARRINGTON EVENT

The last great geomagnetic storm was in 1859, called the "Carrington Event" after the astronomer who noted the phenomenon. The 1859 great geomagnetic storm caused fires in telegraph stations and burned the just-laid transatlantic cable, but its effects were not catastrophic because electronic systems were few and not essential to society in 1859. Great geomagnetic storms are recognizable in historical records because they produce highly unusual effects, like the appearance of the Aurora Borealis at the equator, that even common people often record in letters and diaries. No great geomagnetic storm has occurred in the modern era, in which society depends for its very existence on electronics. Most specialists believe a great geo-magnetic storm is overdue, since this once-a-century phenomenon last occurred in 1859. Many scientists believe a great geomagnetic storm is most likely to occur during the solar maximum, when solar flares and coronal mass ejections that cause geomagnetic storms increase sharply in frequency. The solar maximum recurs every 11 years, the last in 2012–2013.

NASA and the National Academy of Sciences (NAS) published a blue-ribbon study independently confirming the warning of the EMP Commission about the threat posed by a great geomagnetic storm. The EMP Commission and the NASA reports, and several subsequent independent studies, conclude that if a great geomagnetic storm like the 1859 Carrington Event happened today, millions could die.

NON-NUCLEAR EMP WEAPONS

Radiofrequency weapons of widely varying designs —some using conventional explosions to generate an EMP, others using microwave emitters to direct energy at a target, for example—can destroy, damage, and disrupt electronic systems at short ranges. Non-nuclear EMP weapons seldom have ranges or a radius of effect greater than 1 kilometer, and usually much less than this.

Some scientists credibly claim that non-nuclear EMP weapons can be developed having a radius of effect of tens of kilometers. However, no nation has yet demonstrated such a capability, including the United States, which has worked to develop advanced radiofrequency weapons for many years. Even such advanced non-nuclear EMP weapons would still be limited and localized in their effects, compared to the Nation-wide effects of a nuclear EMP attack or the planetary effects of a great geomagnetic storm.

Microwave radiation is the lethal mechanism usually employed by non-nuclear EMP weapons, an effect somewhat comparable but not identical to E1 from a nuclear weapon. Radiofrequency weapons produce no E2 or E3 pulse.

Terrorists, criminals, and even lone individuals can build a non-nuclear EMP weapon without great trouble or expense, working from Unclassified designs publicly available on the internet, and using parts available at any electronics store. In 2000, the Terrorism Panel of the House Armed Services Committee sponsored an experiment, recruiting a small team of amateur electronics enthusiasts to attempt constructing a radiofrequency weapon, relying only on Unclassified design information and parts purchased from Radio Shack. The team, in 1 year, built two radio-frequency weapons of radically different designs. One was designed to fit inside the shipping crate for a Xerox machine, so it could be delivered to the Pentagon mail room where (in those more unguarded days before 9/11) it could slowly fry the Pentagon's computers. The other radiofrequency weapon was designed to fit inside a small Volkswagen bus, so it could be driven down Wall Street and disrupt computers—and perhaps the National economy.

Both designs were demonstrated and tested successfully during a special Congressional hearing for this purpose at the U.S. Army's Aberdeen Proving Ground.

Radiofrequency weapons are not merely a hypothetical threat. Terrorists, criminals, and disgruntled individuals have used home-made radiofrequency weapons. The U.S. military and foreign militaries have a wide variety of such weaponry.

Moreover, non-nuclear EMP devices that could be used as radiofrequency weapons are publicly marketed for sale to anyone, usually advertised as "EMP simulators." For example, one such simulator is advertised for public sale as an "EMP Suitcase." This EMP simulator is designed to look like a suitcase, can be carried and operated by one person, and is purpose-built with a high energy radiofrequency output to destroy electronics. However, it has only a short radius of effect. Nonetheless, a terrorist or deranged individual who knows what he is doing, who has studied the electric grid for a major metropolitan area, could— armed with the "EMP Suitcase"— black out a major city.

THE NUCLEAR EMP ATTACK

Emphasis is warranted that the nuclear EMP threat is not merely theoretical— it is real, a clear and present danger. Nuclear EMP attack is the perfect asymmetric weapon for state actors who wish to level the battlefield by neutralizing the great technological advantage enjoyed by U.S. military forces. EMP is also the ideal means, the only means, whereby rogue states or terrorists could use a single nuclear weapon to destroy the United States and prevail in the War on Terrorism or some other conflict with a single blow. The EMP Commission also warned that states or terrorists could exploit U.S. vulnerability to EMP attack for coercion or blackmail: "Therefore, terrorists or state actors that possess relatively unsophisticated missiles armed with nuclear weapons may well calculate that, instead of destroying a city or military base, they may obtain the greatest political-military utility from one or a few such weapons by using them—or threatening their use—in an EMP attack."

The EMP Commission found that states such as Russia, China, North Korea, and Iran have incorporated EMP attack into their military doctrines, and openly de-scribe making EMP attacks against the United States. Indeed, the EMP Commission was established by Congress partly in response to a Russian nuclear EMP threat made to an official Congressional Delegation on May 2, 1999, in the midst of the Balkans crisis.

Vladimir Lukin, head of the Russian delegation and a former Ambassador to the United States, warned: "Hypothetically, if Russia really wanted to hurt the United States in retaliation for NATO's bombing of Yugoslavia, Russia could fire an SLBM and detonate a single nuclear warhead at high altitude over the United States. The resulting EMP would massively disrupt U.S. communications and computer systems, shutting down everything."

China's military doctrine also openly describes EMP attack as the ultimate asymmetric weapon, as it strikes at the very technology that is the basis of U.S. power. Where EMP is concerned, "The United States is more vulnerable to attacks than any other country in the world."

"Some people might think that things similar to the 'Pearl Harbor Incident' are un-likely to take place during the information age. Yet it could be regarded as the 'Pearl Harbor Incident' of the 21st Century if a surprise attack is conducted against the enemy's crucial information systems of command, control, and communications by such means as . . . electromagnetic pulse weapons . . . Even a superpower like the United States, which possesses nuclear missiles and powerful armed forces, cannot guarantee its immunity . . . In their own words, a highly computerized open society like the United States is extremely vulnerable to electronic attacks from all sides. This is because the U.S.

economy, from banks to telephone systems and from power plants to iron and steel works, relies entirely on computer networks . . . When a country grows increasingly powerful economically and technologically . . . it will become increasingly dependent on modern information systems . . . The United States is more vulnerable to attacks than any other country in the world."

Iran—the world's leading sponsor of international terrorism—in military writings openly describes EMP as a terrorist weapon, and as the ultimate weapon for prevailing over the West: "If the world's industrial countries fail to devise effective ways to defend themselves against dangerous electronic assaults, then they will disintegrate within a few years . . . American soldiers would not be able to find food to eat nor would they be able to fire a single shot."

The threats are not merely words. The EMP Commission assesses that Russia has, as it openly declares in military writings, probably developed what Russia describes as a "Super-EMP" nuclear weapon—specifically designed to generate extraordinarily high EMP fields in order to paralyze even the best protected U.S. strategic and military forces. China probably also has Super-EMP weapons. North Korea too may possess or be developing a Super-EMP nuclear weapon, as alleged by credible Russian sources to the EMP Commission, and by open-source reporting from South

Korean military intelligence. But any nuclear weapon, even a low-yield first generation device, could suffice to make a catastrophic EMP attack on the United States. Iran, although it is assessed as not yet having the bomb, is actively testing missile delivery systems and has practiced launches of its best missile, the Shahab–III, testing for high-altitude detonations, in exercises that look suspiciously like training for making EMP attacks. As noted earlier, Iran has also practiced launching from a ship a Scud, the world's most common missile — possessed by over 60 nations, terrorist groups, and private collectors. A Scud might be the ideal choice for a ship-launched EMP attack against the United States intended to be executed anonymously, to escape any last-gasp U.S. retaliation. Unlike a nuclear weapon detonated in a city, a high-altitude EMP attack leaves no bomb debris for forensic analysis, no perpetrator "fingerprints."

EMP VULNERABILITIES

Today's microelectronics are the foundation of our modern civilization, but are over 1 million times more vulnerable to EMP than the far more primitive and robust electronics of the 1960s, that proved vulnerable during nuclear EMP tests of that era. Tests conducted by the EMP Commission confirmed empirically the theory that, as modern microelectronics become ever smaller and more efficient, and operate ever faster on lower voltages, they also become ever more vulnerable, and can be destroyed or disrupted by much lower EMP field strengths.

Microelectronics and electronic systems are everywhere, and run virtually every-thing in the modern world. All of the civilian critical infrastructures that sustain the economy of the United States, and the lives of 310 million Americans, depend, directly or indirectly, upon electricity and electronic systems.

Of special concern is the vulnerability to EMP of the Extra-High-Voltage (EHV) transformers, that are indispensable to the operation of the electric grid. EHV transformers drive electric current over long distances, from the point of generation to consumers (from the Niagara Falls hydroelectric facility to New York City, for example). The electric grid cannot operate without EHV transformers—which could be destroyed by an EMP event. The United States no longer manufactures

EHV transformers. They must be manufactured and imported from overseas, from Germany or South Korea, the only two nations in the world that manufacture such transformers for export. Each EHV transformer must be custom-made for its unique role in the grid. A single EHV transformer typically requires 18 months to manufacture. The loss of large numbers of EHV transformers to an EMP event would plunge the United States into a protracted blackout lasting years, with perhaps no hope of eventual recovery, as the society and population probably could not survive for even 1 year without electricity.

Another key vulnerability to EMP are Supervisory Control And Data Acquisition systems (SCADAs). SCADAs essentially are small computers, numbering in the millions and ubiquitous everywhere in the critical infrastructures, that perform jobs previously performed by hundreds of thousands of human technicians during the 1960s and before, in the era prior to the microelectronics revolution. SCADAs do things like regulating the flow of electricity into a transformer, controlling the flow of gas through a pipeline, or running traffic control lights. SCADAs enable a few dozen people to run the critical infrastructures for an entire city, whereas previously hundreds or even thousands of technicians were necessary. Unfortunately, SCADAs are especially vulnerable to EMP.

EHV transformers and SCADAs are the most important vulnerabilities to EMP, but are by no means the only vulnerabilities. Each of the critical infrastructures has their own unique vulnerabilities to EMP:

The National electric grid, with its transformers and generators and electronic controls and thousands of miles of power lines, is a vast electronic machine — more vulnerable to EMP than any other critical infrastructure. Yet the electric grid is the most important of all critical infrastructures, and is in fact the keystone supporting modern civilization, as it powers all the other critical infrastructures. As of now it is our technological Achilles Heel. The EMP Commission found that, if the electric grid collapses, so too will collapse all the other critical infrastructures. But, if the electric grid can be protected and recovered, so too all the other critical infrastructures can also be restored.

Transportation is a critical infrastructure because modern civilization cannot exist without the goods and services moved by road, rail, ship, and air. Cars, trucks, locomotives, ships, and aircraft all have electronic components, motors, and controls that are potentially vulnerable to EMP. Traffic control systems that avert traffic jams and collisions for road, rail, and air depend upon electronic systems, that the EMP Commission discovered are especially vulnerable to EMP. Gas stations, fuel pipelines, and refineries that make petroleum products depend upon electronic components and cannot operate without electricity. Given our current state of unpreparedness, in the aftermath of a natural or nuclear EMP event, transportation systems would be paralyzed.

Communications is a critical infrastructure because modern economies and the cohesion and operation of modern societies depend to a degree unprecedented in history on the rapid movement of information— accomplished today mostly by electronic means. Telephones, cell phones, personal computers, television, and radio are all directly vulnerable to EMP, and cannot operate without electricity. Satellites that operate at Low-Earth-Orbit (LEO) for communications, weather, scientific, and military purposes are vulnerable to EMP and to collateral effects from an EMP attack. Within weeks of an EMP event, the LEO satellites, which comprise most satellites, would probably be inoperable. In the aftermath of a nuclear or natural EMP event, under present levels of preparedness, communications would be severely limited, restricted mainly to those few military communications networks that are hardened against EMP.

Banking and finance are the critical infrastructure that sustain modern economies. Whether it is the stock market, the financial records of a multinational corporation, or the ATM card of an individual— financial transactions and record keeping all depend now at the macro- and micro-level upon computers and electronic automated systems. Many of these are directly vulnerable to EMP, and none can operate without electricity. The EMP Commission found that an EMP event could transform the modern electronic economy into a feudal economy based on barter.

Food has always been vital to every person and every civilization. The critical infrastructure for producing, delivering, and storing food depends upon a complex web of technology, including machines for planting and harvesting and packaging, refrigerated vehicles for long-haul transportation, and temperature-controlled warehouses. Modern technology enables over 98 percent of the U.S. National population to be fed by less than 2 percent of the population. Huge regional warehouses that resupply supermarkets constitute the National food reserves, enough food to feed the Nation for 30–60 days at normal consumption rates, the warehoused food preserved by refrigeration and temperature control systems that typically have enough emergency electrical power (diesel or gas generators) to last only about an average of 3 days. Experience with storm-induced blackouts proves that when these big regional food warehouses lose electrical power, most of the food supply will rapidly spoil. Farmers, less than 2 percent of the population as noted above, cannot feed 310 million Americans if deprived of the means that currently makes possible this technological miracle.

Water too has always been a basic necessity to every person and civilization, even more crucial than food. The critical infrastructure for purifying and delivering potable water, and for disposing of and treating waste water, is a vast networked machine powered by electricity that uses electrical pumps, screens, filters, paddles, and sprayers to purify and deliver drinkable water, and to remove and treat waste water. Much of the machinery in the water infrastructure is directly vulnerable to EMP. The system cannot operate without vast amounts of electricity supplied by the power grid. A natural or nuclear EMP event would immediately deprive most of the U.S. National population of running water. Many natural sources of water—lakes, streams, and rivers—would be dangerously polluted by toxic wastes from sewage, industry, and hospitals that would backflow from or bypass wastewater treatment plants, that could no longer intake and treat pollutants without electric power. Many natural water sources that would normally be safe to drink, after an EMP event, would be polluted with human wastes including industrial wastes and arsenic and heavy metals, and hospital wastes including pathogens.

Emergency services such as police, fire, and hospitals are the critical infrastructure that upholds the most basic functions of government and society— preserving law and order, protecting property and life. Experience from protracted storm-induced blackouts has shown, for example in the aftermath of Hurricanes Andrew and Katrina, that when the lights go out and communications systems fail and there is no gas for squad cars, fire trucks, and ambulances, the worst elements of society and the worst human instincts rapidly takeover.

EMERGENCY FOODS AND WATER PURIFICATION

When you are picking out the items to stock your emergency larder with, you want to make certain that you have a good assortment of different foods so that your diet is balanced and you can avoid the mental fatigue of eating the same bland meals endlessly. Calorie intake is also very important to keep in mind for emergency food supplies, as keeping your energy up is important. Everything from dried meat to grains to Jell-O can be included in your food store, and probably should be – if it can be stored for a long while, it has a place on your shelves unless you hate it or are allergic to it. Your survival food store should include the following types of food:

- **Grains**– both wheat and corn fall into this category, for flour and corn meal respectively. These can be stored whole and ground, or as flour. Whole grains keep better but are more work to prepare. Included in this category are also various mixes – you can include pancake mix, pie crust mix, and even cake mixes in your grain supply as long as you also have some means of cooking them to the proper temperature.

- **Meats**– a combination of dried meats and tinned meats, as well as canned fish, for the essential proteins that the carnivore known as man requires. Tuna and sardines will last for a minimum of three years in their tins, and provide a lot of essential nutrients. Be sure to have a can opener so that you can open them easily. The author has witnessed Russians opening a stout tin can with a knife – it works, but it produces frequent sliced fingers even among those skilled at doing it.

- **Beans and sprouts**– you should have several types of beans, and possibly the material for sprouts as well.

- **Dairy products**– powdered milk and powdered eggs are the only dairy products you will be able to store over the long-term.

- **Sugars**– actual sugar, as well as hard candy, chocolate powder for cocoa or drink mix, and honey, which is an excellent long-lasting food resource but should not be given to small children. White sugar keeps indefinitely, confectioner's sugar and granulated sugar will last two to three years, and brown sugar lasts around 18 months.

- **Fruits and vegetables**– either dried or canned, these are essential for proper nutrition. Shelled nuts only last a few months before going stale, but those left unshelled will stay edible for at least two years.

- **Condiments and miscellaneous foods**– salt, pepper, onion powder, powdered or dried tomatoes, and whatever spices you enjoy, preferably in quantity and variety. Jell-O and other gelatin or pudding mixes can keep for a year or two. Teabags will keep for around three years, so you can sip a placid, civilized cup of Lipton's or Earl Grey even while the world burns around you. Ritz crackers and Peanut Butter are a basic long-term storage staple.

MREs - Made ready to eat

History of the MRE:

The Meal, Ready-to-Eat is also known as an MRE. It is self-contained in light weight packaging and used in the United States military. The MRE replaced the Meal, Combat, Individual (MCI) rations. Because of the range geographic tastes, the Department of Defense began to design MREs that would suit many different cultures.

The goal of an emergency food supply is to have enough calories to survive until other food sources arrive so it is important that the service member eat the entire meal. This did not always happen if the meal did not seem palpable to the person consuming it. Vegetarian options have now been added.

There are no laws that forbid the resale of MREs. They can be found on survival and disaster websites and were used in for the victims in Hurricane Katrina and other disasters where there was a shortage of food.

MRE Meals Contents may include:

- Main course or entree
- A side dish
- Dessert or snack
- Crackers or bread
- Spread of cheese, peanut butter or jelly

- Powdered beverage mix: fruit flavored drink, cocoa, instant coffee or tea, sport drink or dairy shake.
- Utensils (usually just a plastic spoon)
- Flameless Ration Heater (FRH)
- Beverage mixing bag
- Accessory pack:
  - Xylitol chewing gum
  - Water-resistant matches
  - Napkins
  - Seasonings include salt, pepper, sugar, creamer and Tabasco sauce.

Many items are fortified with nutrients. In addition, the Department of Defense policy requires units to augment MREs with fresh food and A-Rations whenever feasible, especially in training environments.

Nutritional requirements

- Each meal needs to provide 1,200 calories
- Each has a shelf life of 3 years depending on storage
- It is not recommended that MREs be consumed for more than 21 days in a row

Water storage and purification

When planning your water resources for survival you need to deal with storing water, finding water and purifying water.

Storing Water

For your in-home cache or survival retreat stash, you should count on two gallons of water per-person per-day. While this is more water than necessary to survive (except in hot climates or after strenuous exertion) it ensures water is available for hygiene and cooking as well as drinking.

Our personal in-home stash has enough water for a week.

Commercial gallon bottles of filtered/purified spring water often carry expiration dates two years after the bottling date. A good rotation program is necessary to ensure your supply of water remains fresh and drinkable.

If you have a spare refrigerator in the basement or the garage, use PET water bottles (the kind soda or liters of water come in) to fill any available freezer space. In addition to providing you with fresh, easily transportable drinking water, the ice can be used to cool food in the refrigerator in the event of a power failure. We have found that these bottles, which are clear and have screw-on caps like soda bottles, will withstand many freeze-thaw cycles without bursting or leaking. (The bottom may distort when frozen, but this isn't a big problem.) For self-storage of large amounts of water, you're probably better off with containers of at least 5 gallons. Food-grade plastic storage containers are available commercially in sizes from five gallons to 250 or more. Containers with handles and spouts are usually five to seven gallons, which will weigh between 40 and 56 pounds. Get too far beyond that and you'll have great difficulty moving a full tank.

Solutions designed to be added to water to prepare it for long-term storage are commercially available. Bleach can also be used to treat tap water from municipal sources. Added at a rate of about 1 teaspoon per 10 gallons, bleach can ensure the water will remain drinkable.

Once you're in a survival situation where there is a limited amount of water, conservation is an important consideration. While drinking water is critical, water is also necessary for rehydrating and cooking dried foods. Water from boiling pasta, cooking vegetables and similar sources can and should be retained and drunk, after it has cooled. Canned vegetables also contain liquid that can be consumed.

To preserve water, save water from washing your hands, clothes and dishes to flush toilets.

Short Term Storage

People who have electric pumps drawing water from their well have learned the lesson of filling up all available pots and pans when a thunderstorm is brewing. What would you do if you knew your water supply would be disrupted in an hour?

Here are a couple options in addition to filling the pots and pans:

- The simplest option is to put two or three heavy-duty plastic trash bags (avoid those with post-consumer recycled content) inside each other. Then fill the inner bag with water. You can even use the trash can to give structure to the bag. (A good argument for keeping your trash can fairly clean!)

- Fill your bath tub almost to the top. While you probably won't want to drink this water, it can be used to flush toilets, and wash your hands.

If you are at home, a fair amount of water will be stored in your water pipes and related system.

To get access to this water, first close the valve to the outside as soon as possible. This will prevent the water from running out as pressure to the entire system drops and prevent contaminated water from entering your house.

Then open a faucet on the top floor. This will let air into the system so a vacuum doesn't hold the water in. Next, you can open a faucet in the basement. Gravity should allow the water in your pipes to run out the open faucet. You can repeat this procedure for both hot and cold systems.

Your hot water heater will also have plenty of water inside it. You can access this water from the valve on the bottom. Again, you may need to open a faucet somewhere else in the house to ensure a smooth flow of water. Sediment often collects in the bottom of a hot water heater. While a good maintenance program can prevent this, it should not be dangerous. Simply allow any stirred up dirt to again drift to the bottom.

Finding or Obtaining Water

There are certain climates and geographic locations where finding water will either be extremely easy or nearly impossible. You'll have to take your location into account when you read the following. Best suggestion: Buy a guide book tailored for your location, be it desert, jungle, arctic or temperate.

Wherever you live, your best bet for finding a source of water is to scout out suitable locations and stock up necessary equipment before an emergency befalls you. With proper preparedness, you should know not only the location of the nearest streams, springs or other water source but specific locations where it would be easy to fill a container and the safest way to get it home.

Preparedness also means having at hand an easily installable system for collecting rain water. This can range from large tarps or sheets of plastic to a system for collecting water run off from your roof or gutters.

Purification

And while you may think any water will do in a pinch, water that is not purified may make you sick, possibly even killing you. In a survival situation, with little or no medical attention available, you need to remain as healthy as possible.

Boiling water is the best method for purifying running water you gather from natural sources. It doesn't require any chemicals, or expensive equipment -- all you need is a large pot and a good fire or similar heat source. Plus, a rolling boil for 20 or 30 minutes should kill common bacteria such as guardia and cryptosporidium. One should consider that boiling water will not remove foreign contaminants such as radiation or heavy metals.

Outside of boiling, commercial purification/filter devices made by companies such as PUR or Katadyn are the best choices. They range in size from small pump filters designed for backpackers to large filters designed for entire camps. Probably the best filtering devices for survival retreats are the model where you pour water into the top and allow it to slowly seep through the media into a reservoir on the bottom. No pumping is required.

On the down side, most such filtering devices are expensive and have a limited capacity. Filters are good for anywhere from 200 liters to thousands of gallons, depending on the filter size and mechanism. Some filters used fiberglass and activated charcoal. Others use impregnated resin or even ceramic elements.

Chemical additives are another, often less suitable option. The water purification pills sold to hikers and campers have a limited shelf life, especially once the bottle has been opened.

Pour-though filtering systems can be made in an emergency. Here's one example that will remove many contaminants:

1. Take a five or seven gallon pail (a 55-gallon drum can also be used for a larger scale system) and drill or punch a series of small holes on the bottom.

2. Place several layers of cloth on the bottom of the bucket, this can be anything from denim to an old table cloth.

3. Add a thick layer of sand (preferred) or loose dirt. This will be the main filtering element, so you should add at least half of the pail's depth.

4. Add another few layers of cloth, weighted down with a few larger rocks.

5. Your home-made filter should be several inches below the top of the bucket.

6. Place another bucket or other collection device under the holes you punched on the bottom.

7. Pour collected or gathered water into the top of your new filter system. As gravity works its magic, the water will filter through the media and drip out the bottom, into your collection device. If the water is cloudy or full of sediment, simply let it drop to the bottom and draw the cleaner water off the top of your collection device with a straw or tube.

While this system may not be the best purification method, it has been successfully used in the past. For rain water or water gathered from what appear to be relatively clean sources of running water, the system should work fine.

CONCLUSIONS

Semper Paratus – Always Ready

The EMP Commission found that, given our current state of unpreparedness, a natural or nuclear EMP event could create anarchic conditions that would profoundly challenge the existence of social order. The time to prepare is now – the means to prepare is knowledge. This book is a one-of-a-kind dossier on all aspects of surviving EMP events. Thank you for ordering this book and if you have a chance, leave a good review on Amazon!

My website contains more information and other books:

http://writers-web-services.com

BIBLIOGRAPHY

Captain Dave's News & Views – Food and Water. Accessed June 29, 2017. http://captaindaves.com/.

Congress.gov | Library of Congress. Accessed June 29, 2017. https://www.congress.gov/114/crpt/srpt250/CRPT-114srpt250.pdf.

"Planet X News | Guest Writer David Meade Bio and Articles." Planet X News. Accessed June 29, 2017. http://planetxnews.com/meade/.

Milton Keynes UK
Ingram Content Group UK Ltd.
UKHW040859140124
435980UK00004B/82